THE FREEDOM FORMULA

How to free yourself from debt and reclaim your life

Carl Hill

Published by www.lulu.com

For Tamara

CONTENTS

INTRODUCTION

- Do you find you have less and less time to do the things you enjoy?

- Do you worry that your lifestyle is damaging the planet?

- Do you find that no matter how hard you work you never seem any better off financially?

- Do you wonder how you will cope in times of economic down turn?

- Do you wonder whether you will ever be really happy?

If so, then this guide is for you.

Consider the following facts:

- We are working long hours, often in unsatisfying jobs.

- Our lifestyle is destroying the planet.

- We pay thousands of pounds in interest on ever increasing debts.

- Increasing our material consumption has not made us happier.

These facts suggest something about how we live is going drastically wrong, but what? We all need to earn and spend money to a certain extent, but maybe its time to assess exactly why we do this. Maybe the received wisdom about how and why we earn and spend money is simply incorrect. So why earn and spend at all?

Firstly, you need to satisfy your needs such as food, clothing, somewhere to live etc. In other words, the basics. You will also want to satisfy some needs beyond the basics. What these are will vary from person to person.

Some people couldn't live without music, so a good stereo and CDs would, for them, be a need. Some people enjoy socialising regularly, so for them, a weekly night out with friends would constitute a need. These requirements may not be necessary in order to live a "normal" life, but they are the things that make life worth living. You may be able to survive without them, but life would certainly seem a lot duller.

Secondly, you earn money to satisfy your wants. These are things that you don't really *need* such as clothes you rarely wear, or CDs you never listen to. It is not essential that you have these things; you have them because you want them. They provide a certain amount of pleasure (or the act of buying them did) but no-where near as much as the things you really need.

Still, it seems logical that you should satisfy as many wants as possible. Who wouldn't opt for two holidays instead of one? Who wouldn't enjoy a new car every year instead of every four or five? The more wants that you can satisfy, the better your life will be. In theory "more is better." All very logical so far. It stands to reason that in order to satisfy more wants you will have to earn more money to pay for them, so, following this logic, the more money you earn the better your life will be.

You can earn more money by either working more hours at your current rate of pay, or working the same hours on a better rate of pay. Either way you will have to work harder. The company you work for is not going to pay you any more than it has to, because that would reduce its profits and what company

8

would deliberately do such a thing? It will only pay you more if you produce more, and therefore increase its income to cover the extra cost. So you can work longer hours to increase the amount you earn for your company or you could maybe get promoted, taking extra responsibility, and so earn more money for your company through the decisions you make on its behalf. Alternatively you could borrow the extra money and temporarily increase your income.

This working harder, to earn more, to buy more, results in a process represented in the following diagram:

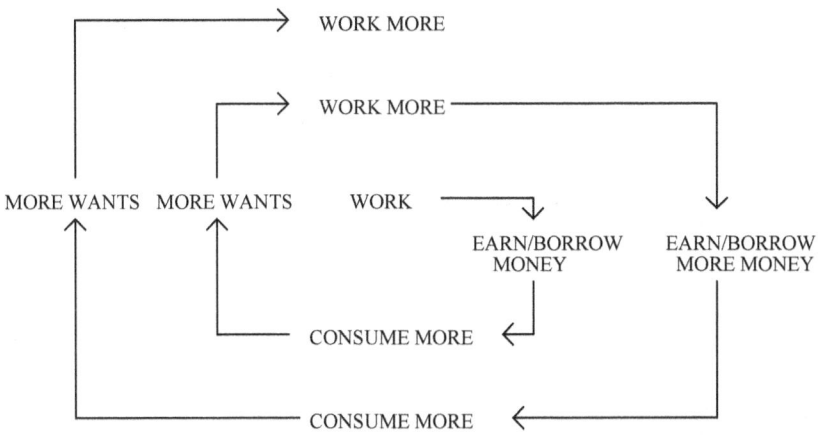

As the diagram shows, each time you work more, you earn more and therefore you can satisfy more wants. However, at this point your wants increase to compensate for the extra work you are doing. You may decide to book an extra holiday because you are working hard, but you only need an extra holiday because you work so many hours and you will have to work more hours to pay for the holiday. You may decide to take a loan to buy a car, but the extra work you need to do to pay the interest on the loan will probably take up more time than the bus ride you were trying to avoid. So, in turn, you work or borrow more again, and so on.

No matter how hard you work or how many wants you satisfy, you can never reach a point of complete satisfaction due to this compensatory effect. In both instances you will be effectively back where you started, no better off (and financially worse off) and still needing another holiday, or another car. The price you pay for the satisfaction of wants - is more wants!

This process ensures that you work more, to earn more, to consume more. This is detrimental from a personal point of view because you are spending more time at work, financially because you will owe more money and from an environmental point of view because more resources are being used when your consumption increases. Remember, it has been shown that this increase in consumption rarely raises happiness levels.

So, how can this process be broken? We all need to earn money to pay for our needs but what can we do about our wants? Consider the next diagram

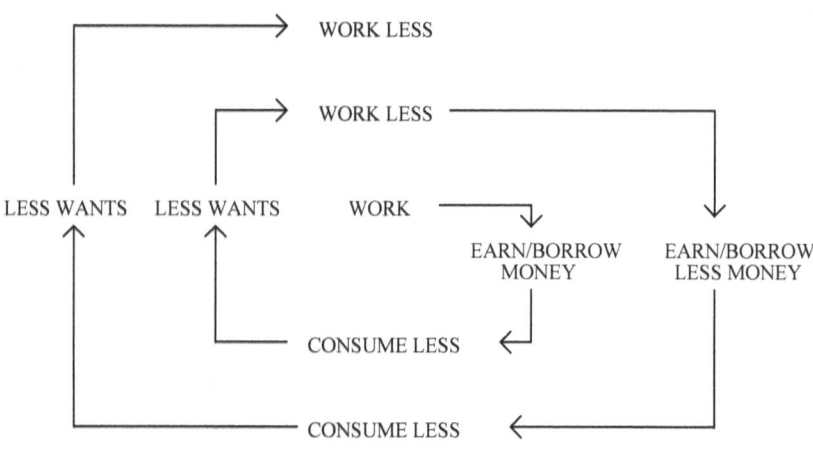

You will notice that this diagram looks very similar to the first but works in exactly the opposite way. It also doesn't seem as "natural", in that it doesn't appear to represent how people actually act. This is because the process represented by the first diagram makes the basic assumption that more is better. The second, however, assumes that less is better, and this assumption is rarely made.

Why not reduce the number of holidays you take? It will save you money and you can then have extra time away from work every week. You will enjoy the occasional holiday more as well, because you will not be exhausted. Why not cycle to work instead of driving? It will save you money and you will not have to make time to go to the gym.

This alternative process demonstrates that by consuming less you are able to earn less, which means you could spend less time at work and use fewer of the planets resources.

Of course, a large number of people work a set number of hours and so cannot simply increase or decrease their hours of work as and when they wish. However, more and more companies are now offering flexible working patterns and this makes it possible for you to rearrange your working hours. Equally, a lot of people work overtime on a purely voluntary basis, which means that they can revert to working just a standard week if they wish. Opportunities to arrange your own hours are increasing as companies discover the benefits of "flexible working patterns". How does not working overtime or working part time sound? Good? Then read on, its perfectly possible.

But remember, even if reducing your working hours is easily arranged, it can still be very difficult to stop the first process once it has started. This is because the powers that be have a huge interest in maintaining it. What would happen to tour operators if everyone halved the number of holidays they booked? What would happen to car manufacturers if everyone cycled to work? What would happen to the governments tax revenues if everyone worked and spent less? Every time you work your company pays you only a proportion of the money you have actually generated for it. The difference between what you earn for your company and what they actually pay you is the company's profit (how else could they make a profit?). Every time your company pays you , you have to pay tax on your earnings. Every time you spend that money you pay tax on the item you buy. You also pay more for the item than it is actually worth because the shop has to make a profit too. At every point in the first process someone

11

else is making money. It should come as no surprise that this process (and the corresponding environmental damage) is promoted as the norm. A norm for who's benefit? Not yours!

The second process, however, starts to give you back control over more aspects of your life, and this means that you no longer have to pay as many people to do that controlling for you. If you work less, buy less and do more for yourself, you can decide what your money is spent on, as opposed to having this decided for you by others who are only too happy to charge you for the privilege. This is because you now have time to decide and do things for yourself. You could cook instead of buying ready meals. You could research and book your own holiday instead of paying a travel agent to do it for you. The second process also means that an employer hasn't the hold on you they would have, if you needed a particularly well paid job to service your debts. Being able to switch employers without any significant loss of benefits puts you in a position where you can choose where to work, and means you will not have to fall in line with any particular employer's opinions or policies. In other words, you have the power to argue or leave.

Remember that the second process is not the norm. Expect strong reactions from some (generally those who are most caught in the first spiral). 'Miser', 'drop-out', 'slacker', 'waster' - get used to these "insults" and take them as compliments. They are the voice of a "norm" that wants you back.

HOW THIS GUIDE WORKS

Part 1 - This section gives a set of general principles that support the second process and compares them to the generally held assumptions supporting the first process. Think of them as a new way of perceiving money and work, one that is normally hidden.

Part 2 - This section gives practical hints and tips on how to decrease your spending. They are not specific, but aim to promote further investigation rather than dictate exactly what you should do. Use the internet to research the areas.

If you don't have internet access then your public library can provide it, or the relevant books. Some ideas you may want to try, others not - no one would want to follow them all. They provide a starting point from which you can discover the thousands of possibilities for reducing your consumption and improving your life.

Read the whole guide through without doing anything to see how it works as a whole. It is deliberately short, as is your time, so shouldn't take long! Then go back and read it again, this time putting the ideas into practice.

PART 1

CHAPTER 1 - THE MAIN PRINCIPLES

MORE THAN YOU NEED IS WORTHLESS

Imagine it is a hot day. You are thirsty and you come across a shop selling cold drinks. You notice, however, that the drinks are being sold at double their normal price. Do you buy one? Probably, if you are thirsty enough. Now imagine the same scenario, but this time you are not thirsty. Do you still buy one? Probably not, you aren't thirsty, so you can wait until you find somewhere selling the drinks at their normal price.

In both scenarios the drink was the same price but the choice you made was different. Your choice differed because the amount you "needed" the drink differed. If we stop for a moment and imagine that we applied this test to everything we buy, we begin to see that money is worth more if we spend it on things we need. It buys us more satisfaction than if we spend it on things we just want. The wants represent a bad deal, because for the same amount of money you get less satisfaction.

Beyond the point of need, therefore, consumption becomes an increasingly bad deal. The generally held point of view, however, is that the more we consume the more satisfied we will be. More holidays are good. More cars are good. But the above example proves that the exact reverse is true. The more we own the less satisfaction it gives. Taken to it's logical conclusion we can see that the continued satisfaction of a want would eventually make the wanted item worthless.

Consider the case of a man who owns ten cars. The purchase of another car is unlikely to make him any more satisfied since he is unlikely to need his ten cars, let alone an eleventh. Now think about the first time you bought a car and how much satisfaction you felt from just that one car. In our heart we know that owning more things cannot continually give more satisfaction, but we continue to believe the myth and act accordingly. We adhere to the first process, but for whose benefit is this process working?

We can ensure that our money is well spent, therefore, by buying only those things that we need.

CONVERT PRICE IN POUNDS TO HOURS WORKED

We all earn money at different rates. One person can earn £15.00 net (after tax and national insurance deductions) for an hour's work and another only £7.50. The cost of goods bought is the same in pounds for both people, the cost to each person, however, is different.

We get money by selling "chunks" of our lives to our employer. For the time we are at work we cannot live life as we would want; we are required to live life in accordance with our employer's wishes. That is what a job is. Our employers want us to make money for them, and a proportion of this money is then paid to us in the form of a salary. This salary is then converted into the goods that we require when we spend it. So the real cost to each person is how many "chunks" of their life they have to sell to buy any given thing.

Say a CD costs £15.00 pounds. That's one hours work for the first person who earns £15.00 per hour, but two hours work for the person who earns £7.50. The CD is the same for both people, it costs the same in pounds for both people. The real cost to each however, is different.

You can find the real cost of any item by working out your net hourly rate of pay. You can do this with a recent payslip. Try to ensure you use one from a typical week or month to make sure the figures are as accurate as possible and not distorted by sick pay or unusual overtime etc. Take your net pay (your take home pay after all deductions for tax etc) and divide it by the number of hours worked during the pay period.

So, say you are paid £1150.00 net in a month, that's £13,800 net a year approximately (on a salary of £20,500 gross year). If you work 35 hours a week that's 1820 a year. Your net hourly rate is £13,800.00 divided by 1820 = £7.50 approximately.

Write this figure down and remember it.

Each time you buy an item, divide its price in pounds by the figure you worked out above. This will give you the item's real price, i.e. the number of hours of your life you had to sell in order to buy it. You may think nothing of buying a CD every week, but after working out it's real cost you discover that you have to work for two hours to earn the money to buy it. Would you rather work two hours a week less or buy a CD every week?

By applying this calculation you will find that your decisions regarding purchases begin to change. Armed with the real cost of an item, you can make an informed choice about whether it is worth the amount of work required to pay for it. Equally, by following the second process you can limit what you buy in order to take back the "chunks" of you life you no longer need to sell.

CREDIT IS DEBT

Have you noticed that people do not use the word "debt"? The more acceptable phrase, is "credit". When we think of "debt" we have visions of collectors at the door, repossessions and struggling to make ends meet. When we think of "credit" we imagine gold cards, loan agreements and shopping. These two pictures are radically different but, of course, "debt" and "credit" are exactly the same thing.

Today, debt is extremely common. Credit cards, loans and hire purchase schemes are all offered to us on a daily basis. They enable us to buy things without actually having the money to pay for them. In return, we pay interest on the debt. This interest makes the credit companies a lot of money. This profit is the reason why credit is so heavily promoted.

From your point of view as the purchaser, however, debt means you will be paying a lot more for the item than if you bought it for cash. You pay this extra amount (in the form of interest) for the convenience of being able to buy something you can't instantly afford. You will be working part of every week to earn enough money to cover the interest. This extra work is actually buying you nothing.

One area where debt is necessary is house purchase. It is as good as impossible to save enough money to buy a house out-right, since inflation will eventually force house prices up faster than you are able to save. This problem is compounded by the requirement to pay rent in some form until you buy a house, therefore reducing the amount you can afford to save. Rent, just like interest, actually buys nothing.

For everything other than a house, however, it is worth saving the money to make the purchase so that you avoid paying interest. If you are tempted to get into debt, then remember to make your decision based on the amount you will actually pay for the item, including interest. This is often shown as "Total amount payable" on loan quotations. The price of the item is not the real price unless this is taken in to consideration. Compare this price to the cost of the item if you paid for it in cash. Now calculate the difference, and convert this difference into hours worked. This is what the debt will really cost you.

Saving money will be made a whole lot easier by the other tips in this book. This will make the necessity of debt less likely.

LOOK AFTER THE PENNIES

"Look after the pennies and the pounds will look after themselves." An old saying that turns out to be strangely appropriate. It is easy to see why saving twenty or thirty pounds, and the corresponding time at work, would be to your advantage, but why save a pound or fifty pence? The corresponding time at work is almost negligible. But, as the saying above points out, those pounds and fifty pence's add up to a significant amount of work when considered over time.

Say, for example, you buy lunch each day at work. You go to a shop that is near by, and this shop (because of it's convenient location) charges £5.00 for a sandwich. Another shop, ten minutes walk away, charges £4.00. The ten minute walk therefore saves you £1.00 a day. This is about £20.00 month, or £240.00 a year. If you are paid £7.50 an hour it equates to 32 hours work. This is about a weeks work for a ten minute walk each day. Effectively this could mean an extra weeks holiday a year and, you'll be a bit fitter and more relaxed after the walk!

Now what seemed like a negligible amount becomes significant. Reducing your regular spending by even a small amount can significantly reduce the amount of work you have to do.

REFUSE TO BE SOLD ANYTHING

Few products are bought, most are sold. Millions of pounds are spent selling products via such methods as advertising, market research and training sales staff. None of this money, though, goes into making the product any better. The cost of all this selling will, however, be included in the price of the product. The more a product is sold, therefore, the worse deal it represents, since more of the money you pay for it has gone into selling rather than producing it.

As a buyer, your aim is to get the product at the cheapest price possible. The aim of those selling is to get the highest price possible. These objectives will always conflict. In other words, the person selling the product will always actively oppose your main aim of trying to get the cheapest price for the product. The image portrayed, however, will be the exact opposite. The sales person will always present themselves as being on your side. Always remember that this is not the case and the sales person is only concerned with making the sale.

Below are some of the most common techniques to look out for:

1. Products are sold by appealing to you as an individual. For example, the same car will be sold as "sporty" to a young single man but "reliable" to a female pensioner.

2. Friendliness is just a cover for finding out information about you. For instance, the answer to "Did you get here okay?" could tell the sales person where you live or whether you own a car. This information will then be used to a build a picture of you so the product can be sold in a way that appeals to you.

3. The product will normally be sold before the full price is given. Once you have committed to buying the item, extras will be added on. Delivery, handling charges, insurance etc. These are normally hidden by the much used "Prices from" phrase. Make sure that you get a full price at the very start of the conversation.

4. If you refuse to buy the product then be prepared. A good sales person will know the main reasons why customers do not buy and will have prepared arguments against them. Examples include "I can only get you this price today," "There is only one left in stock," etc.

5. The best way to avoid these sales traps is to avoid sales environments. Many products can be found in "Best Buy" lists of consumer magazines or internet sites. These allow you to decide on a product without any sales pressure. Then shop around, taking details away from the shops you visit to look at in your own time. Only go to buy a product once you have decided what you want, at what price and from where. That way your decision is based

on what *you* want and not what the sales person wants.

ASK A GRANNY

In many societies the elderly are seen as an asset. They are a valuable source of knowledge and provide a link between past and present. In western societies, because of our emphasis on work, the elderly are seen as a burden. "We" have to pay for "Them" by working.

Many elderly people know how to live very well on very little. They probably did not have the material possessions that we now all take for granted, but they lived perfectly well just the same. Ask them how they did this, they will be only too pleased to tell you. Knowledge of how to mend clothes, grow vegetables, make cold remedies and more will all be available. In the process of finding this information you will make them feel valued.

LOOK AFTER THE PLANET

Western economies are built on the assumption of economic growth. The idea is that if we produce more, people consume more, and if people consume more then other people get richer and the economy grows. The fatal flaw in this process is that to produce more we need to use more natural resources and although economic growth is, in theory, infinite, the Earth's capacity to deal with the pollution caused by this increased production and consumption is not. The most obvious sign of this is climate change.

Think about what actually goes into producing something simple like a mug. There is the energy needed to extract and transport the raw materials, the energy needed to make it, the energy needed to transport the goods to a warehouse or shop, the energy you use getting to and from that shop. Then think of all the energy you used to earn enough money to pay for the mug! And that's just a mug! Try following the argument for a car or computer..

We can reduce our environmental impact by using less resources to live in the same way, ie. by following the first process. We can be more energy efficient and recycle materials, for example. Much of the gains made from these steps are, however, outweighed by the underlying economic growth. No matter how efficient we become we will be fighting a losing battle because we will continue to use more and more resources to drive that growth.

The only way we can realistically halt the damage we are doing to the environment is by consuming less. In other words, by following the second process. Why not do yourself and the planet a big favour?

CHAPTER 2 - CLEAR YOUR DEBTS

Any debt will have interest charged on it. You are not just paying back what you owe, but paying for owing that money as well. As explained in the previous chapter, paying interest on debts is a bad deal because you are getting nothing in return for this expenditure. Interest payments make up a huge amount of people's expenditure but most people are not aware of just how much. If you want to be able to work less you need to clear all your debts and in so doing reduce your expenditure.

But first a note about rent. Renting is even worse than credit because you paying for something that you will never actually own. The rental amount is effectively a never ending interest payment. Even though you pay more if you buy on credit, eventually you will own the item you have bought. This is not the case for renting because you will go on paying rent indefinitely. In all the following calculations therefore, if you rent your property, the payment should be noted on a 100% interest rate and the normal payment taken as the payment amount.

We will all have debts to varying degrees, so your first task is to know exactly where you stand. Check all your rental or credit agreements, your mortgage/rent, loans, credit cards etc and note the following information. The company name, the amount currently outstanding, the APR rate (annual percentage rate i.e. interest) and your monthly payment . If you do not have this information or your latest statement is an old one, ring the companies and request an up to date statement. Balances and interest rates change monthly so it is important to have the correct figures. Once you have these, list all your debt in a table like the one that follows. Put the highest APR rated debt at the top (remember any rental payments will be 100% APR) and move down to the lowest APR.

Company Name	Balance Outstanding	APR (interest Rate)	Monthly Payment
Rent (if no mortgage)	Rent	100.00%	650.00*
Store Card	£1,500.00	18.00%	£55.00
Credit Card	£3,000.00	15.00%	£105.00
Car Loan	£15,000	8.00%	£305.00
Mortgage (if not renting)	£110,000.00	5.00%	650.00*
Total	£129,500.00	n/a	£1,115.00

Once you have done this, total the last column headed "Monthly Payments". Divide this figure by your net pay (as worked out in chapter 1). So, taking the total monthly payment above of £1,115.00 and dividing it by the figure worked out at £7.50 - £1,115.00 divided by £7.50 = 150 approximately. This figure represents the number of hours per month that you work just to pay your debts. The table above has been calculated using average household debts, you may notice that on an average wage, the debt payments are nearly equivalent to the average monthly income. In other words, the average debt repayments take up the whole salary of an average income person working full time! This is why most households need two full time workers to survive. Now the real cost of debt is beginning to show itself. This is how much time you could gain per year if you paid off all your debts.

The idea is to clear your debts as soon as possible. You will need to reduce your other outgoings to allow you to pay off your debts sooner. This will have the effect of gradually reducing your monthly debt payments (because you have less debt outstanding) which in turn will give you more money to pay any remaining debts. It may seem an impossible task initially because of the amount of debt that needs to be cleared, but this book aims to show you that it *is* possible, and can be done a lot quicker than you think. You do not have to be in debt!

REARRANGE YOUR EXISTING DEBTS

This is probably the easiest way to save money, but the one that most people ignore. The idea is to make sure that you pay as little interest as possible on what debt you do have. Your mortgage or rental payments may well require some major alterations to your finances and will be covered later. For now, we will concentrate on the easiest way to save money. Check the APR rates on your debts. You will probably notice they vary considerably. Normally the lowest rates will be charged on anything secured against a property (mortgage, home loans etc) followed by personal loans, credit cards, and finally store cards. Now look at moving the higher APR debts to the lower ones. For example, you could move a store card balance onto your standard credit card (or a new one with 0% deal) or move all your card balances onto a loan. You could even move all credit onto a loan secured against your property if your house is worth enough to cover your mortgage and an extra loan. You could do this at the same time as re-arranging your mortgage (see below). If you do this remember to ensure that any credit you do swap remains on its original number of years (i.e. it finishes no later than the original debt would have), otherwise you can wipe out any saving you make on the interest rate by paying it over a longer period of time.

One possible way of saving money is by switching your mortgage company or "re mortgaging". Some lenders offer very good deals if you switch to them. You can find a lower interest rate for a set period, and get legal and valuation fees refunded or paid for. Remember, however, to check the current rate you are paying first; you may find that you are on your lenders "standard variable rate" it may be that this cannot be beaten by another lender. Also beware of any tie in periods that mean you have to remain with the company after any deal has finished. This means that you will not be able to switch your mortgage again after your deal has finished, for a set period of time. Equally do not be tempted to borrow more money when you switch (unless it is to consolidate debts currently on a higher rate of interest). Finally, make sure you start to shop around before your deal ends so you are prepared to switch again if a higher interest rate kicks in. By switching from lender to lender, and taking advantage of their deals, you can save thousands of pounds. Most people cannot be bothered. This is what lenders count on and it is how they make their profits. Follow the guidelines for arranging a new mortgage below to help you choose which re mortgage offer to go for.

Once you have moved all your debts to the lowest rate possible, get rid of any cards or agreements that have been cleared. "Empty" credit cards are nothing more than temptations to spend on the assumption that you will pay them off the next month. This of course never happens, and you can end up having moved the balance and created a whole new one as well! You think you have enough will power to resist? Ask yourself two questions: Did you plan to have such a high balance on credit cards in the first place? And, how come credit card companies make so much money?

STOP RENTING

As pointed out before, rent is effectively 100% interest because you never pay the debt off. The most commonly rented item is a house. There was a time, when for most ordinary people renting a house was the only option because they simply didn't have the income to cover a mortgage, and mortgages were very difficult to get. This is not the case any more. So, what will you need to get one?

1. Firstly, you will need a reasonable credit history. This means that if you have any arrangements to clear debts you had difficulty paying, then these must be cleared first. Use the information offered in the rest of this book to help you

decrease your outgoings and pay the extra saved off any outstanding bad debt. Once you have cleared it, ensure the company sends you a letter confirming this to be the case, as it can take some time for the computer records to be updated and you may need proof. Retain copies of this.

2. Secondly, you will need a deposit. This means you will need some money of your own to put towards the house purchase. The amount will normally be 10 or 15% of the purchase price. So if you are buying a house for £175,000 you will need at least £17,500 of your own before you are able to borrow the other £157,500. Again, if you haven't got a deposit, follow the guidelines in this book to help you save the money or consider a shared equity scheme (see below).

3. Finally, you will need an income that is enough to cover the mortgage payment. This criteria is normally set by the lender but is approximately 3 to 4 times your gross annual income (that's what you earn in a year before any tax, national insurance or pensions are taken off). This figure is stated on your P60 form, which you receive yearly from the Inland Revenue, or can be obtained from your employer. So if you earn £40,000 (jointly or on your own) then you can probably borrow about £120,000 - £160,000 depending on your other outgoings.

If your income isn't enough to buy a house then there are several things you can do.

1. Firstly, you can reduce your other debts thereby giving you more to spend on a mortgage (most responsible lenders work on disposable income - that is the amount you have left from your income after you have paid any other debts) and so increasing the amount you can borrow.

2. You could take a part time job to boost your earnings and increase the amount you can borrow.

3. You could buy with other people and share the house.

4. Purchase a "shared ownership" property. This is an arrangement where you buy say 50% of the house and rent the other 50% from a housing association, with a view to paying for the remaining 50% when you can afford it. This is a way of buying a house if your income is not enough to buy outright.

5. Shared equity schemes work in a similar way. You buy a share in the property, but rather than renting the remaining part, the seller retains a share which he redeems (along with any related rise in the shares value) on sale. Of course, you will benefit from any rise in value of your share if you sell, and the scheme provides a low cost way of entering the housing market even though you do not entirely own the property,

Do not be tempted to borrow money from lenders who do not check your income, credit history, or insist on a deposit (so called 'non-status' lending). They will almost certainly charge you a huge amount of interest due to the extra risk they are taking on you repaying the loan. Remember, if a reputable lender doesn't think you can afford a mortgage, then the chances are you can't. A mortgage is secured on your property, which means if you don't pay, for whatever reason, the lender can repossess your house and sell it to repay your mortgage.

ARRANGING A NEW MORTGAGE

So, assuming you meet these criteria, how do you choose which mortgage to take? The best way to decide is to check a finance magazine or web site, which will list all lenders according to a variety of criteria such as cost, service, early repayment penalties etc. This way you can narrow down your choices to a few of those recommended, and get quotes from those to compare. Do the same for any associated house insurance or life assurance, as they are generally sold along with the mortgage. You do not, however, have to have these all with the same company! Don't worry if the companies you choose don't have a branch near you, as most places will accept applications via the internet, phone or post with perhaps a final visit to sign paperwork etc.

Whichever mortgage you choose, you must ensure that you do not pay penalties for paying extra on top of your normal mortgage payment (remember the idea is to clear the mortgage as quickly as possible and reduce the total interest paid). Some mortgages only allow a set amount to be paid in addition to your normal payment each month without penalty so you must ensure you do not exceed this. If you have additional money spare over and above this additional amount then it is better to save the extra in a savings account until the penalty period has finished and then make a lump sum reduction. Remember, anyone you speak to will try to sell you the mortgage which is most advantageous to the company, not the mortgage that is most advantageous to you.

FINDING A PROPERTY

After you have chosen which mortgage and insurances to take, and have a rough idea of how much you can borrow, its time to find a property. It is worth bearing in mind that this is likely to be the biggest financial commitment you will ever make, so take your time! Remember that the smaller the mortgage the quicker you will be able to pay it off - the mortgage size is likely to depend on three main things: the size of the property, where it is and it's condition (i.e. If it needs repairs/modernisation).

1. When it comes to house size most people think that bigger is better, but this is more to do with status than need . If you ask most people why they require a bigger house they will say that they "need more space", but for what? That extra space will normally be filled with things that rarely get used. Every house has a loft, so who wants to pay an extra £20,000 on a mortgage (and the associated interest!) for storage space? Think carefully about what size house you really need. Remember that a bigger house will mean bigger heating bills, higher community charge and more expensive maintenance.

2. The area in which the property is situated will effect it's price dramatically. Moving a few streets away, whilst making no practical difference to where you live, can shift you from "area x" to "area y", adding thousands to the price of a property. Moving away from town centres and into the suburbs often means more space, better views and subsequently higher property prices. It also means

however, that you will be further away from amenities and so you are likely to have to drive or use public transport to get to them, both of which cost time and money. It is worth considering moving within easy reach of local amenities because of this, and house prices will often be cheaper as a result.

3. Older houses can offer more space for less money but often lack modern fittings such as double glazing or central heating. If you can have these installed cheaply enough it is worth considering as an option. If not however, you will probably spend more money improving the property than you would if you bought one that had already been modernised. Equally, older properties are more likely to need running repairs, and so will prove more expensive to maintain

Whatever you decide, there are some general points to consider.

1. Make sure you visit the property both during the day and at night, to inspect it and to see what the area is like at different times.

2. Ask neighbours a few doors away from the property what they think of the area, or about any problems they encounter; they will have a more objective point of view than the people selling the property.

3. You may also want to make a surprise visit to the property to see what it is like under normal circumstances.

4. Also, make sure that you test any appliances such as heaters or cookers which are to be included in the purchase.

Most people will advertise the property at about 5% higher than it is worth, and expect to negotiate, so start by offering 10% less than the asking price. Ignore phrases such as "There are other people interested," or "We can't afford to accept less than the asking price." These are often used to persuade you to make a hasty decision. Only pay what you think the house is worth.

It is worth considering these points even if you own your property already - could you downsize and cut your expenditure that way?

Now you have basic mortgage information and have found the property, all that is left for you to do is to go back to your chosen lender and apply for the mortgage. At this stage, make sure you stick to your original plan; it is, after all, the adviser's last chance to improve his sales figures, and its easy to panic when you have decided to take on such a large commitment. Remember, the decisions you made whilst shopping around will still apply now.

CLEARING THE DEBT

So at this stage you should have reduced your rental agreements as much as possible or cleared them entirely and you have rearranged any existing debt to make sure you are paying as little as possible. The next step is to ensure that you do not increase this debt. It is unlikely, once you have gone to all this trouble, that you will use credit to pay for any unnecessary extras you may want - but what about unexpected essentials? What if the car breaks down or you need a new water tank? The best planning in the world will not avoid the unexpected happening and to cover this you need to save an "emergency fund".

How much you save is up to you but as a rough guide you should have about three times your monthly income. Save this first before paying anything off your debts and remember that at some point you will need to use it so you will need to keep it topped up. A good way of doing this is to prepare to spend about a months income every year (some years it will be more, some years less, but this should balance out), so you need to save towards this amount on a monthly basis. You need to save a twelfth of one months income each month. If your household net income (that is the total earnings for everyone in the house) is £2300.00 a month you will need to save £2300.00 divided by 12, which equals about £190.00, per month.

So how much, in total, do you actually spend in a month? The only way to know this is to write it all down. Write down everything you spend for a whole month and that means everything: petrol, lunches, chocolate bars, a couple of drinks after work, write it all down no matter how small. Check your bank statements for regular outgoings such as utility bills and food shopping and remember to add a monthly figure (your annual spend divided by 12) for annual

31

costs such as holidays and Christmas. Then you can add this up at the end of the month and complete a table as in the example over page.

You will need to add categories for expenditures that don't fit any particular category because, of course, each person's list will be different. The important aspect is that every thing is included. Now subtract this figure from your net income. So if you, as a household, earn £2300.00 then you need to take your total outgoings away from this to leave your "disposable" (i.e. unaccounted for) income. This figure is likely to come as a shock because you are either going to wonder where this money normally disappears to, or you may find you have very little left. Read on to find out how you can ensure there is something left and that what remains is used productively.

Look back at the table you made of your debts. Your main priority should be to clear the debt with the highest APR figure first, as this is costing you the most (apart from rent which you can't clear with additional payments of course). Add your spare income, what ever it is (£10.00 or £100.00), to your monthly payment on this debt. This will have a dual effect; it will clear the debt quicker and substantially reduce the interest you pay. Eventually the debt will be cleared and your monthly payment will finish. This payment can then be added to your disposable income and this higher amount is in turn used to reduce the next debt even faster. This snowball effect works a lot quicker than most people realise because of the reduction of interest paid. Eventually you will probably be left with just your mortgage as a debt and can add all of your disposable income to your mortgage payments. This will substantially reduce both the term of your mortgage and the interest paid over that term.

NET HOUSEHOLD MONTHLY INCOME	£2,300.00

DEBTS

RENTAL (If no mortage) *		650.00*
100% interest as rented		
STORE CARD		£55.00
£1500 over 3 years at 18.00%		
CREDIT CARD		£105.00
£3000.00 over 3 years at 15.00%		
LOAN		£305.00
£1500.00 over 5 years at 8.00%		
MORTGAGE (If not renting)*		650.00*
£110,000 over 25 years at 5.0%		
TOTAL DEBT PAYMENTS		£1,115.00

COSTS

HOUSEHOLD COSTS	£200.00
TRANSPORT	£100.00
HOLIDAYS (£1200 ANNUAL BUDGET)	£100.00
CLOTHES/PERSONAL	£75.00
FOOD & DRINK	£250.00
HEALTH	£20.00
ENTERTAINMENT	£125.00
MISCELLANEOUS	£25.00
EMERGENCY FUND TOP UP	£190.00

TOTAL COSTS	£1,085.00

TOTAL OUTGOINGS	£2,200.00

DISPOSABLE INCOME	£100.00

CHAPTER 3 - HOW MUCH CAN YOU SAVE?

So how much difference does this actually make? Lets look again at the table of expenditure from Chapter 2. What would happen, for example, if you could reduce this expenditure by just £100.00 per month?

So, for example, you make an extra payment of £100.00 on to your store card which, once its cleared, leaves £155.00 (the £55.00 payment plus the £100.00 extra) to pay off your credit card. Once this is cleared, you use the £155.00 from the store card plus the £105.00 from the credit card's normal payment to pay an extra £260.00 extra off your loan and so on. By doing this you can save thousands of pounds in interest. The more you pay off your debts the bigger the saving becomes. What would happen if you reduced your expenditure by £500.00 a month ? Unlikely but not impossible! Take a look at the following table which gives figures for additional payments of £100.00 and £500.00. It shows the interest paid on the debts, the revised interest paid and, crucially, the corresponding savings. More importantly consider the equivalent working hours. Assuming a household net income of £15.00 per hour, in paying the standard payment on a £110,000.00 mortgage, a total of 5527 hours will have to be worked to pay the interest alone. That's 158 weeks! Increasing the payment by £100.00 reduces this to 4040 hours, 115 weeks and increasing by £500 reduces this to 2000 hours, 57 weeks.

	Mortgage £110,000	Loan £15,000
Standard Monthly Cost	£650.00	£305.00
Standard Interest Paid	£82,915.00	£3,249.00
Standard Repayment Term	25 YEARS	5 YEARS
Monthly Cost + £100	£750.00	£405.00
Revised Interest Paid	£60,614.00	£2,247.00
Revised Repayment Term	19 YEARS	2 YEARS 6 MONTHS
Interest Saved	£22,301.00	£1,002.00
Monthly Cost + £500	£1,150.00	£805.00
Revised Interest Paid	£30,006.00	£834.00
Revised Repayment Term	10 YEARS	1 YEAR 7 MONTHS
Interest Saved	£52,909.00	£2,415.00

	Credit Card £3000.00	Store Card £1500
Standard Monthly Cost	£105.00	£55.00
Standard Interest Paid	£744.00	£452.00
Standard Repayment Term	3 YEARS	3 YEARS
Monthly Cost + £100	£205.00	£155.00
Revised Interest Paid	£320.00	£135.00
Revised Repayment Term	1 YEAR 4 MONTHS	11 MONTHS
Interest Saved	£424.00	£320.00
Monthly Cost + £500	£605.00	£555.00
Revised Interest Paid	£109.00	£45.00
Revised Repayment Term	5 MONTHS	3 MONTHS
Interest Saved	£635.00	£410.00

*note figures are approximate for ease of illustration

- The more you reduce your expenditure, the more you can pay off your debts.

- The more you pay off your debts, the quicker you clear them.

- The quicker you clear them, the less interest you pay.

- The less interest you pay, the less you have to earn.

- The less you have to earn, the less you have to work.

- The less you have to work, the more you can live your life.

In Part 2 there are hints and tips for reducing expenditure. Remember that even a £10.00 saving will make a difference and, once you start using the process outlined in the previous chapters, the possibilities are endless. The tips given are just that, and will need some further investigation on your part. You will find some of the tips useful and others not, so there is little point giving lengthy information about them all. This makes the lists quick to read and allows you to get on with implementing them instead of reading about them.

PART 2

MAXIMISING YOUR SPARE INCOME
CHAPTER 4 - PERSONAL FINANCE

Your money has to be somewhere between your earning and spending it. That somewhere will more than likely be a current or savings account. In either case you will be earning interest on your money and paying for certain services so it makes sense to maximise the amount of interest you earn and decrease the charges you pay.

1. Move your current account. Check a finance magazine or web-site for best-buy tables and choose one with the highest interest rate and lowest charges. Your existing and new banks are obliged to sort out the transfer out for you.
2. Move any spare money out of your current account to a savings account, (the interest will be far higher), or put the money into National Savings where you don't earn interest as such but are entered into a prize draw. With interest rates being low, you can often earn more than in an account with a guaranteed interest payment.
3. Put the spare money into an account which is tax free but which gives you the access you need. This could be withdrawals at any time; once a month, or once a year depending on what the money is used for. Consider splitting the money into separate funds with maybe an instant access account for money regularly used, and an account allowing one or two withdrawals a year for your emergency fund or holiday money etc.

4. Financial advice can be useful but ensure you take such advice from several sources for comparison and remember to buy only what you originally planned. Financial advisers are highly trained salesmen and often receive commission, so they will be keen to maximise their sales.

5. Beware the investment that promises untold riches in five years or more - this type of investment does not normally guarantee back what you put in, let alone any actual interest. On top of this there are often charges enforced for "managing" this type of account which you pay out of the money in the account. Remember, if it sounds too good to be true, then it is!

6. Get a pension. It is doubtful if the sate pension enjoyed today will be available in the future so you need to make your own provision. The earlier you do this the cheaper it is so, whatever age you are, make arrangements to set up a pension. If possible, join a company scheme, as your employer is required to pay into the scheme to top up your contributions. This increases the amount you have in your pension fund. They also give you a projection of how much your pension will be worth on retirement, although this can be changed at any time! If you can't join a company scheme then you will need to set up a private pension. As before check the best buy tables, shop around and beware of salesmen.

7. Loyalty cards are very popular and offer discounts for shopping at particular stores. To ensure you get good value from these you need to convert the points into pounds and then knock that amount off the price of the item you are buying. Compare this price to other stores before purchase. For example you may get 50 points if you buy something worth £5.00 and those 50 points may equate to 25p. So you are actually paying £4.75 for the item. If somewhere else is selling the same thing for less than £4.75 it makes sense to buy it from there.

8. If you use loyalty cards, then make sure you get one for every shop - they are called loyalty cards for a reason - they encourage you to buy from one shop only. Get a card for all the shops you use and enjoy the discount without being trapped by "loyalty".

9. Some stores will offer a discount if you open a credit card with them. This

may be significant if you are making a large purchase. Take out the card and receive the discount (make sure you only buy what you would have bought without the card or you will end up worse off). Once you receive the first statement, pay off the balance and cancel the agreement.

CHAPTER 5 - HOUSEHOLD COSTS

A good proportion of your income will be spent on household costs. This is reasonable because your house is the biggest thing you own, but equally, this means it is an area where big savings can be made.

1. One of your biggest costs will be for energy. Check who you are buying your energy from and compare different companies to see if it is worth switching providers. If you do not have internet access at home your local library will. You will need your latest bill and information on units used to do this.

2. Reduce the number of electrical appliances you use. Dry clothes on a line not in a tumble dryer. Only wash a full load and on a low temperature. Do you need a microwave, when all you use it for is defrosting things? Anything you think you can live without put on a "trial period" and don't use it for a month. If you don't use it, sell it or give it away.

3. When you buy a new appliance check its has the highest energy efficiency rating.

4. Replace light bulbs with low energy versions when they break. They cost more but last longer and use a fraction of the energy.

5. Turning off lights when not in a room and turning the heating down to a minimum when you are not in causes you no inconvenience yet saves you money.

6. Make sure your house is well insulated: loft insulation, draft proofing doors and windows and other simple measures can save you 30% on your heating

bills. Check your local library for DIY books about insulation and check with your local council for energy grants as some will contribute to the cost of these improvements.

7. Don't site your fridge next to the cooker as it will have to work harder to remove the heat it gains when the cooker is on.

8. Make sure curtains are tucked behind radiators so the heat goes into the room and not out of the window.

9. Use lids on saucepans to reduce boiling time and use only the amount of water you need.

10. If you are not on a water meter then get an estimate of how much your bill would be with one. Without one you will pay a set price no matter how much you use, so cant save money by reducing your consumption.

11. Most water is used in the bathroom. A shower uses a fraction of the water of a bath. Leaving the tap running while brushing your teeth uses 5 litres, while a dripping tap can use up to 30 litres a day!

12. Buy a specially designed toilet flush handle to restrict the amount of water used to flush or you can save flush water by putting an empty drinks bottle in the cistern.

13. Do you need a landline telephone if you have access to a phone at work or if you already have (and intend to keep) a mobile?

14. Compare telephone providers online and inform your existing provider that you are thinking of changing. They will review your payment plan based on the number and times of calls you make and may be able to make a saving for you.

15. Ask yourself if you really need a mobile phone. How often are you away from, or cant get to, a phone?

16. Swap your mobile tariff to "pay as you go" so you only pay for the time you use.

17. House insurance for both your building and contents is often included in your mortgage payment but this may not be the cheapest policy. Check what you are covered for by looking at the policy document and write down what you need. Contact a broker or look at best buy tables in a financial magazine or

web-site to find a cheaper alternative.

18. Another area of household cost is maintenance. Maintenance is essential to prevent small jobs turning into bigger jobs and small bills into bigger bills! Make a check list of maintenance areas such as windows, seals, pipes, water tanks, roof tiles etc. and check through it every year so that any faults can be picked up early.

19. Buy a good DIY manual that covers all the basics. This means that you will be able to tackle simple jobs yourself. If you do, it is worth buying materials from a trade suppliers and not from big DIY stores.

20. If you need to call an expert do not just choose the first person in the phone book. Check the local press for smaller adverts (they cost less so you should be charged less) or better still ask around family or friends for a recommendation.

21. Make sure you get quotes from at least three different companies before agreeing to any work being done.

22. Ensure that any tradesmen you use are properly qualified and certified by a professional body, that way you can be more certain that the work will be of a good standard and you can report any that isn't to the appropriate body.

23. When buying large items for the house such as appliances and furniture, try to buy the best quality you can afford. These are not necessarily the most expensive! Good quality items last longer and so prevent you having to replace them.

24. Take care of appliances. Read the maintenance part of any instruction manual and follow it.

25. If you cannot afford to buy good quality items from new, consider buying second hand.

26. When buying decorative items such as pictures or ornaments look for the cheapest. They are not required to "do anything" so do not need to be made to last, and they are likely to be the things you change if you redecorate.

27. Don't buy a multitude of specific cleaners. One multi-surface cleaner should be sufficient for most cleaning jobs.

28. An even cheaper alternative is to make your own cleaners. Bicarbonate of

soda makes an excellent scourer, white wine vinegar will clean glass and ceramics and olive oil can be used to polish wood.

CHAPTER 6 - TRANSPORT

The mode of transport you use will depend upon a number of factors. The most important of these being distance. You can, for instance, travel further on a bike than on foot and further on a bus than on a bike. This may sound obvious but because we live in a world designed for cars, the car is often our chosen mode of transport. This does not mean it is the either the quickest or cheapest.

1. Match your mode of transport to the journey. Do you need to drive to the local shop when you could walk in ten minutes? Do you live close enough to your workplace to cycle at least some of the time?

2. Buy from your local shops instead of the supermarket. The products may be (although not necessarily) a little more expensive, but don't forget you are paying for a car to get you to the bigger stores and this effectively adds to the cost of your shopping.

3. Consider using public transport. Season tickets often give discounts and can prove very economical when compared to the cost of buying, running and parking a car.

4. If you need a car then, again, check the best buy tables. Buy the smallest engine size available as this will be cheaper to run and insure. Remember extras such as air conditioning or electric windows add to the price of the car and are very expensive to repair if they fail.

5. If you are buying a new car then wait until the current registration is due to finish as this is when special deals such as discounts and free insurance will be available. If you require a loan to buy the car remember that the finance offered by the garage is rarely the cheapest available.

6. If you are buying second hand then it is imperative that someone who knows about cars checks the vehicle before you buy it if you can't do this yourself. If you don't know anyone who can do this, then it is worth paying a fee to a motoring organisation to check the car before you buy.

7. Remember to add any finance taken to your list of debts and remember that schemes where you can constantly "trade up" to a new model after a few years are effectively rental agreements and to be avoided.

8. Major work can often be avoided by ensuring smaller maintenance work is carried out regularly. Often, with the help of a car manual, you can do these jobs yourself.

9. For major jobs try to find a garage that is recommended by someone you know and make sure you mention their name when you visit so that the mechanic knows your impressions will be passed on to their existing customer.

10. Keep the costs of running a car to a minimum. Washing and waxing your own car is far cheaper than paying for a carwash. Check your tyre pressure is correct as this affects fuel efficiency.

11. Find a cheap garage and keep the tank filled with fuel instead of being caught out and forced to use the first one you come across.

12. Park in the street (even if it means a short walk) rather than paying for car parks. If you have to use a car park, ensure it is long stay or park and ride as it will be a lot cheaper than the city centre equivalents.

13. Drive sensibly. Heavy acceleration and breaking cause huge wear and tear on the car, meaning more repairs. Driving like this also reduces the cars efficiency by using far more fuel.

14. For car insurance, follow the tips given previously for house insurance.

CHAPTER 7 - HOLIDAYS

If you follow the tips in this book you will probably find that your need for holidays decreases. Living on less usually means living more slowly. This reduces your levels of stress and reduces the need to escape your every day life to unwind.

1. Why not holiday at home? Resolve to do nothing that you couldn't do if you were away from home. Equally, make sure you do the things that you would do when you were on holiday. Don't set the alarm, turn off the TV and read, relax on the sofa or in the garden for a whole day, go out for meals instead of cooking. Tell people you are going away in the usual manner, that way they will not be worried if you don't answer calls and they will not be tempted to visit.

2. Before booking a holiday always check an independent guide. These can be found in libraries or on the internet.

3. Roughly speaking, the further you go the more expensive its likely to be. Do you really need to go to the USA when you could go to Europe? Do you need to go to Europe when you could go somewhere in the UK?

4. Consider saving money by travelling by train or ferry instead of flying.

5. If possible, stay clear of times when there is high demand such as school or bank holidays since prices at this time will be much higher (for exactly the same holiday!).

6. Consider camping or staying in a caravan to keep the cost down. Staying in B&Bs is cheaper than hotels.

7. Self catering can be cheaper than staying half or full board but remember to

add on an approximate cost of groceries and any under occupancy charges before comparing.

8. If you decide to stay in a hotel make sure you ask about any special deals that are available (i.e. free extra nights or evening meals).

9. It can often be cheaper to book direct with the main hotel chain by phone or internet rather than ringing the individual hotels, as this is often where the special deals are listed.

10. Bear in mind how much spending money you will need once on holiday. It may be cheap to go camping in Britain, but not if you spend a small fortune entertaining yourselves when it rains every day.

11. It may be expensive, initially, to book into an all inclusive hotel (all drinks and food included) but the cost will be minimal once you are there.

12. Beware of hotels that are some distance from anywhere else as they are likely to inflate their prices, knowing that to go anywhere else is going to mean extra travelling cost for you.

13. Independent guides often give an average price for food and drinks and are worth checking.

14. Rather than booking your holiday as a package try booking the holiday yourself, by contacting airlines or hotels direct, or book a package holiday direct with the tour operator rather than using a travel agent.

15. Book as early as possible if you want to visit a specific resort or hotel as this is when the agents offer maximum discounts.

16. Last minute deals are good value but the choice available can be limited.

17. Ensure you check all the available brochures as they may all feature the same holiday at widely varying prices, and don't forget to add on extras such as flight supplements or under occupancy charges.

18. There are numerous web-sites that will compare prices of different companies for both flights and accommodation.

19. Remember you can pay a high supplement for a good flight but this can be changed at the last minute with absolutely no compensation or refund!

20. Some agents give free travel insurance as an incentive and often you can

request this as part of the deal (try telling them you have been offered the same deal elsewhere with free insurance and you'll normally get it). However if its not included do not buy it. Banks or insurance companies offer the same policies at a much cheaper price and often you can buy a full year policy (covering as many holidays as you take that year) for the same price as a two week policy at the agents.

21. Don't buy your holiday when you first visit, take the details away. Once you have your quote start ringing the other agents and ask them if they can offer the same holiday cheaper. Agents often have a discretionary discount that can be applied but you have to threaten them with going elsewhere to get it.

CHAPTER 8 - CLOTHES AND PERSONAL ITEMS

Practically, clothes serve only one purpose; to protect us from the elements and keep us warm. In reality, however, they also serve many other functions. They define who we are, where we are from, how much money we have or what we do for a living.

The fashion industry is exactly that, an industry. It produces "products" for sale and attempts to charge as much as possible for them. It should be no surprise then, that what is fashionable one year, or season, will not be fashionable the next. It is much more profitable for the industry to constantly sell new clothes than for you to wear the same ones until they actually wear out. This, coupled with the constant appeal of "reinventing" yourself via new clothes, ensures the fashion industry makes huge profits.

1. Disregard fashion and build a wardrobe of well made, practical, classic clothes along with a few cheaper fashion items to keep them up to date.
2. Work out an item's "price per wear". So, for example, a winter coat may cost £200, but if you wear it 100 times the price per wear would be £2. Buying a coat that you only wear 10 times however would work out at £20 per wear. If you only intend to wear something a few times because it is fashionable and will quickly date, then buy the cheaper version.
3. To be able to wear something often enough to justify a high price you will have to ensure it will not wear out and this means looking for quality. Do not, however, think that price automatically equals quality. A specific label may mean a high price but no better quality than a normal high street brand.
4. A label is nothing more than an advert - with you providing free advertising

for the company.

5. Look for natural fibres as they tend to wear better than man-made, check the seams and buttons are all secure and well finished.

6. Always try the clothes on before buying them or ensure you can get a cash refund.

7. Try to avoid dry clean only clothes as much as possible, as the cleaning cost effectively increases the price of the clothes.

8. Remember that clothes have to fit. Buying clothes that are too small because you are planning a diet on Monday is never a good idea; the diet will not materialise and you will be left with unwearable clothes.

9. Sales can be a good way of reducing your clothing cost as long as you disregard the fact that there is a sale on! Don't be tempted by how much an item is reduced, just look at the actual price, and don't buy anything you don't need because it's a good deal, nothing is a good deal if you didn't need it in the first place.

10. Consider second hand clothes from charity shops or friends. These are invariably low cost and can be of good quality.

11. Alternatively look into making your own clothes, this way you can control both quality and price.

12. Once you have bought your clothes it pays to look after them. This means they will wear better and look good for longer. Treat leather with wax, and get shoes reheeled or soled as soon as they begin to wear out. Hang suits and coats correctly and brush them after each wear to help keep them clean. Wash clothes at the correct temperature and make sure you have a stain removal stick handy for emergency use. Any small faults such as split seams or missing buttons should be repaired straight away, ready to wear next time and so as not to cause more damage.

13. Only buy cosmetics that you would normally take on a weeks holiday. This should include all the basics without many extras.

14. Bars of soap will last longer than bottled washes. Stick deodorants will last longer than sprays. Shaving soap will last longer than shaving foams.

15. Cosmetic ranges constantly change. This is to the company's advantage because they get to constantly revise your expectations and so sell you more. Buy effective, simple products to avoid this.

16. Traditional or home branded products are more likely to be cheaper than their highly marketed equivalents. If you don't believe that they contain the same ingredients check the ingredients list and see how similar they are.

17. Don't be fooled into buying "ranges", just because a particular brand of moisturiser works doesn't mean the shampoo will. Resist the urge to maintain brand loyalty and buy whichever product works best for you.

18. Try making your own cosmetics. There are plenty of books or internet sites giving recipes using fresh ingredients and essential oils. You will know exactly what goes into them and you don't pay for the manufacture or marketing.

19. Remember that cosmetics and clothes can only do so much. All the cosmetics and clothes in the world will not hide a hung over face or you being over-weight. The best way to look good is to stay fit and healthy.

CHAPTER 9 - FOOD & DRINK

The well known phrase "You are what you eat" is proving to be true, with more and more links being made between health and diet. The major killers of heart disease and cancer are now known to be influenced by the typical western diet of refined foods; high in fat, sugar and salt and low in essential nutrients. To try and combat this, people turn to fad diets or vitamin supplements instead of simply changing their diet.

Luckily by taking some time and effort to reduce the costs of eating and drinking, the resulting diet is often healthier. Doctors recommend eating more fruit, vegetables and unrefined carbohydrate while cutting down on saturated fat, sugar and salt. The cheaper foods are in fact unrefined carbohydrate such as whole wheat bread, pastas or brown rice, and fruit and vegetables in season. The more expensive foods; meat, dairy and particularly high salt and sugar ready meals are exactly the ones we should be cutting down on. The "bad" news is that to take advantage of this you are going to have to cook.

1. A good way of getting started is to buy a "student" cookbook that gives basic skills and recipes using cheap and easy to find ingredients.

2. Don't buy a lot of specialised cookery books as you may only use one or two recipes from each. Instead, visit the library and copy any recipes you like the look of or cut recipes from magazines. Get a photo album with see-through plastic pages and put the cuttings in to create your own cook book.

3. Don't think that preparing your own meals is restricted to your evening meal. A lot of people disregard lunch, buying sandwiches or snacks to eat at work. It is substantially cheaper to make your own sandwiches, salads or soup

for lunch. If you spend even £4.00 a day on a sandwich that's £20.00 a week, £80.00 a month, £960.00 a year!

4. Supermarkets are sales experts. Large signs declare "special offers", and the displays will be constantly moved so that you have to walk around the entire store and view yet more products. All of this is designed to tempt you into buying more than you need and spending more than you intended.

5. Make a shopping list and stick to it.

6. Don't go shopping when you are tired or hungry because you will be more susceptible to the sales ploys.

7. Supermarkets, however, can be good value for staple items. Tinned foods, rice, milk etc. can all be found very cheaply, particularly if you stick to the "home brand". For anything else however, particularly if the product requires any skills to produce and sell such as bread, meat or fruit and veg, it is better to shop in specialist shops or markets.

8. Fruit and vegetables from a supermarket have often travelled hundreds of miles to get to the store and is therefore days old before you even buy it. This is often countered by chilling the food. By the time you get it home it is already deteriorating and will probably only last a couple of days. Consider buying frozen or tinned produce; although preserved, it is likely to have been processed when fresher. It will almost certainly be cheaper and reduce any waste from fresh produce spoiling before you can use it.

9. Choosing seasonal produce ensures cost is kept to a minimum because the food is readily available. It will therefore be fresher and more nutritious. Find a good greengrocer, market stall or farm shop. Ask where things come from, how to prepare them or whether they have been treated with preservatives. As a rule, for quality and relative cheapness opt as far as possible for seasonal, local and preferably organic produce.

10. Grow your own. A huge amount of produce can be grown in amongst other plants or in containers, fruit trees can be grown against walls to save space, and even a small window box can provide fresh herbs. Alternatively contact your local authority and arrange to rent an allotment.

11. It is better to buy a small amount of good quality meat than a large amount of poor quality. A good butcher will give you advice about preparing and cooking different cuts of meat. More unusual cuts are cheaper and often more tasty as long as they are cooked correctly.

12. Avoid cheap processed meat. You will be cutting down on the amount of fat you eat, as processed meat is often made from parts that couldn't be sold separately ie. the ones you wouldn't want to eat if you knew what they were!

13. When buying meat also bear in mind the condition the animals have been kept in. Organic meat will definitely be more expensive but you will know that the animal has not suffered unnecessarily and has not been routinely drugged with antibiotics (to outweigh the illnesses caused by intensive rearing) or given growth hormones to increase the "product".

14. Try eating a couple of meat-free meals a week by cooking some vegetarian recipes. You will feel the benefit in both your health and your wallet.

15. A good baker will sell a variety of freshly baked goods but they are likely to be a little more expensive than the supermarket standard sliced loaf. Again, the choice is between cost and quality and whether you consider the extra expense worth it.

16. Bear in mind the effect a large supermarket has. They are often sited "out of town" so you have the expense of getting there, they are often so big that they can drive prices down, but this is usually at the expense of variety and quality. Real shops are often driven out of business because they find it impossible to compete, at which point you are left with no choice but to use the supermarket, and this means they can charge exactly what they like because they have a monopoly!

17. Supermarket "premium" ranges may offer better quality and variety. Of course these are offered at "premium" prices to match; prices which are way above those charged by the real high street shops for their "premium" products which they have produced and sold for years!

18. A freezer can be a good investment on two counts. You can buy products in bulk which means they are cheaper, and you can take advantage of any offers

by buying more than you immediately need. Freezers are expensive to run though because they use a lot of energy. Make sure the savings you are making by freezing produce outweighs the cost of running it, by only freezing the more expensive goods which should represent a bigger saving.

 19. If you drink, then you will need to take the cost of alcohol into consideration. One way of keeping this cost down is to buy alcohol when you are on holiday or by making a special trip to buy in bulk. Remember to check the limits for bringing back alcohol from abroad though or you could end up paying a huge amount of duty!

20. Alternatively consider brewing your own alcohol. A trip to the library will supply all the recipes you will need, a lot of which (blackberries, rosehips etc) can be collected for free, making the resulting wine very economical. Wine can also be made from tinned fruits which can be bought very cheaply at supermarkets.

21. Soft drinks are often very expensive, particularly if branded. These brands are just like any other; you are paying for the huge amount of advertising and sponsoring that the company does, you are not paying for the can of sugary water which you actually drink.

22. Bottled water is very expensive when compared to tap water. Try chilling tap water in a bottle and adding some lemon or lime juice to improve the flavour, or invest in a water filter if you are concerned about water quality in your area.

CHAPTER 10 - HEALTH

Many of the changes you make to reduce your expenditure will have a positive effect on your health. Cycling instead of driving, eating fresh food instead of take-aways and generally slowing the pace of life all give your health a boost.

1. Mention exercise, and people immediately think they have to join a gym. Along with this they will need a personal training plan, the latest sports wear, a personal stereo and even "sports" shower gel. But more importantly there is the gym membership fee and the time needed to visit three or four times a week. Is this necessary when all you need to do is exercise?

2. General guidelines recommend three half an hour sessions of exercise per week. Walking or cycling to work would provide the equivalent level of activity in a fraction of the time spent travelling to and being at a gym.

3. Gardening or washing the car by hand all improve your fitness levels.

4. Remember exercise is nothing more than getting your body moving on a regular basis. It should be part of your day to day life, not something to be fitted in and paid for separately.

5. Try exercising at home - hire a library book on exercise routines or buy an exercise DVD (charity shops are full of them around February when all the new year good intentions have been forgotten).

6. If you feel that you need some equipment then buy a set of weights or a skipping rope rather than expensive exercise equipment.

7. If you really do consider that a visit to the gym is essential then try contacting your local leisure centre which will be a lot cheaper than paying a monthly gym membership.

8. One area in which health and economy are undeniably linked is smoking. Smoking not only impacts badly on your health but it also costs a small fortune. There is only one reason people smoke and that's because it is addictive. Visit your doctor and ask their advice on giving up.

9. Another factor that is increasingly being recognised as contributing to ill health is stress. There will always be things that will stress you out so it is useful to counteract this by using a relaxation technique. Each day try to set aside at least half an hour to relax yoga, meditation or tai chi are all popular and numerous books and videos are available on the subjects.

10. When illness does strike, most people's first reaction is to get some medicine to "sort out the problem". This "problem" is seen as external - a bug, an ache, something that has attacked us. The problem with thinking about illness in this way is that it separates "us" from the illness when in fact the illness is part of us. Don't just buy medicine, ask yourself why you are ill and how it can be prevented in the future.

11. Herbal remedies are often cheap and can be self administered. A good guide will give easy to follow recipes such as honey and lemon for a sore throat or elderberry syrup for a cold. These treatments have been used for many years and so are known to be effective with few side effects. Your local health food store will provide plenty of information regarding these treatments, if you don't have one near, try your library or the internet for information.

CHAPTER 11 - ENTERTAINMENT

People often earn more money than they need because they use it to enjoy themselves. This seems reasonable. They work hard to provide the money to do the things they enjoy outside of work. However, the underlying assumption is that the more money they spend the better time they will have. This is sometimes true, but do you need a £50 theme park ticket or a day white water rafting to enjoy yourself? More often than not the over-spending will be just compensating for your lack of time and imagination. Given more time to think about what you want to do and more time to do it, you will find that you need the hit of extreme activities less and reserve them for just a few times a year.

1. There is likely to be a whole range of entertainment provided at low or little cost by your local authority. Check your library or phone your council to get a list of events and get involved in those you might enjoy.

2. Visit your local gallery or museum or take a picnic to your park. Go to the library and read up on your local history so you can visit the places mentioned .

3. Try spending an afternoon browsing in your local library. Consider it the same as surfing the net, looking for bits of information you always wondered about but never got chance to research.

4. If you don't have a computer at home then use the library to access the internet.

5. If you are looking for specific reference information (such as gardening tips or recipes) then why not make up your own file of pages from books in the library by photocopying those of interest and putting them in a photo album.

6. Try looking in charity shops for books or DVDs you intend to buy.

7. By far the most popular form of entertainment is television, and for the cost of a TV and the licence fee, it provides excellent value for money. Ask yourself, however, if you actually need the extra channels provided by satellite or cable as these substantially increase the cost over a year.

8. If you really need a wider choice of programmes then buy a "Freeview" digital receiver or television for a one-off payment.

9. Use your recorder, as this greatly increases the amount of viewing available. Buy a newspaper with a free TV guide, look through it and mark those programmes you would like to watch during the week. You will find that the number you want to record will probably exceed the amount you need without the necessity of extra channels.

10. If you are a music fan, it can prove to be quite an expensive form of entertainment if you buy full-price CDs. Waiting for sales can almost halve your expenditure however and by this time you are likely to have heard more of the CD to know whether its worth buying. You could make a list of the CDs that you want to buy so you can look through sales for them.

11. Don't buy whole albums for just one or two tracks, as you are likely to find these as singles on a compilation album at the end of the year. A particularly cheap way to find these is to buy a "review of the year" music magazine which often come with free CDs.

12. Try looking in charity or second hand record shops for older albums.

13. Use your radio. At practically no cost a radio provides a huge amount of non stop music in every style imaginable.

14. Try traditional games such as chess or dominos, you may be surprised at how engrossing they are. A pack of cards and a book on card games will give a huge variety of options. Board games range from old favourites to modern party games, but once purchased will last a lifetime and require no updating or electricity to enjoy.

15. Gardening is guaranteed to keep you occupied. A garden or even a few window boxes provide contact with plants and the changing seasons, essential in our increasingly man made environment. Ensure that you garden organically

as this saves time in the long run, by nurturing the plants and soil and reducing the need for artificial (and costly) chemical treatments.

16. Make your own compost. Paper, vegetable peelings and grass cuttings can all be composted. You can buy a purpose built composter or make your own from wood, bricks or even a bin liner with holes punched into it.

17. Try to select traditional "cottage garden" plants as these have been around for a long time and so have proven they can withstand the climate, disease and pests. They are also very common so cuttings can be begged from neighbours or, if they have to be bought, they will be easy to find and cheap.

18. Another way to spend time productively is to learn something new. A huge variety of courses are run by education authorities . Whether you want to learn car maintenance or another language you can enrol cheaply and its guaranteed to be nothing like school (i.e. its voluntary and you're paying for it)! Send for a list of courses or attend a college open evening to see if its for you. You could even learn a sport, which has the added advantage of keeping you healthy at the same time.

19. If you do decide to visit the cinema or a restaurant then its worth checking for any special deals. The prices are often drastically reduced if you go at "off peak" times. Details of these special offers can be found in the local press, or you could ring to check the offers. During these times the venues will be less crowded, so you will probably not have to book or wait to be served.

CHAPTER 12 - CONCLUSION

ONCE THE DEBT HAS GONE

So now you have read this guide once, considered some of the ideas, rejected others and probably thought of plenty more yourself, go back to the beginning and start to follow the second process. Your debts will start to come down slowly straight away, and later, as you progress, you will hit the really satisfying period where the debt tumbles away. You will realise that being totally debt free is a realistic possibility. So what happens when you are debt free?

Well, to a certain extent your life will not change. Hopefully you have found that consuming less will have advantages of its own.

- You will be fitter because you are more active.
- You will be more engaged in your local community.
- You will be more in control of your finances.
- You will have learnt new skills.
- You will be living a more environmentally sound life.
- You will be less stressed.
- You will have more time for people.

The biggest advantage, however, is that you only need to work enough hours to cover your new expenditure. This means that far less of your life will be spent at work. You can begin to work part- time.

How much you can reduce your working hours by will depend on how much you have reduced your outgoings. Following the guide in Chapter 1 you will have calculated your net hourly income. You should divide your costs by this amount to work out the number of hours you will need to work. So, for example, your debts are cleared and you have reduced your costs to £750.00 per month. Your hourly household income will be about £15.00 (based on a 35 hour week). Dividing £750.00 by £15.00 gives a total working time of 50 hours per month, which equates to approximately 12 hours a week. Remember this is household income - this could mean one person working 12 hours at £15.00 net per hour or two people working at £7.50 net per hour each.

Part-time was once seen as "not a real job" but things have changed. More and more people are beginning to realise that their work should not be the main priority in life. At the same time employers are realising that part-time workers are more efficient because they are less stressed and offer greater flexibility of working arrangements. A lot of companies offer "Flexi Time" where you are required to work a set number of hours in the week but those hours can be changed to fit in around both you and your employer. Before agreeing to this, however, talk to someone who already does it, as part-time can often mean full time if you are required to cover sick days and holidays.

Your current employer may offer the option of switching from full to part-time or you may take this opportunity to change jobs. If this seems daunting then contact your local Careers Advice Centre who will point you in the right direction.

Whatever you decide to do I hope this guide has shown that we do not have to work for the majority of our lives and consume as much as possible to be happy. In fact we are often far happier if we do exactly the opposite. A slower paced and less materialistic world is a possibility once you look at the options. By earning and spending less you will improve your own life and the lives of others. By working part-time you will give another person the chance of a part-time job. Your impact on our already stressed planet Earth will be greatly reduced. You really can make the world a better place.

Finally, a quote to remember when you are trying to fix the car in the rain, a new recipe sticks to the bottom of the pan or the interest rates go up again: "The journey of a thousand miles begins with just one step." Lao Tzu

www.ingramcontent.com/pod-product-compliance
Lightning Source LLC
Chambersburg PA
CBHW021248280526
45784CB00005B/2284